THE STORY OF **THE**

UNITED STATES

FLAG

BY WYATT BLASSINGAME

PAINTINGS BY VICTOR MAYS

FLAGS BY HENRI A. FLUCHERE

GARRARD PUBLISHING COMPANY
CHAMPAIGN, ILLINOIS

For Phillip Scott
who has seen the flag in far
places and knows what it means

Standard Book Number 8116-4151-1

Library of Congress Catalog Card Number: 69-10030

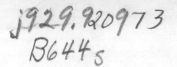

Contents

1. The Great Union Flag

One June morning in 1775 George Washington rode out of Philadelphia. It was a grey day, and a light rain was falling. A few members of the Continental Congress, huddled in their carriages, rode a short distance with the General. With them, on horseback, trotted a group of young men who called themselves the Philadelphia Troop of Light Horse. Their band played, and one of them carried a colorful flag.

This flag was yellow. In the center were pictures of an Indian, a horse's head, and an angel blowing a horn. Far more important, however, was the design in the upper corner next to the flagstaff. This is the part of a flag called the union. Here were thirteen stripes of blue and silver.

We are not sure who designed this flag. But very probably it was the first flag in America to use thirteen stripes to represent the thirteen American colonies.

At this time the American colonies still belonged to Great Britain. But many Americans felt the British government did not treat them fairly. Already three small battles had been fought between British soldiers and the American minutemen. These minutemen were patriotic farmers and businessmen rather than

Minutemen battle the British in this detail from *The Battle of Bunker's Hill* by John Trumbull.

soldiers. But they were the only army the Americans had.

Leaders from the different colonies had just met to form what they called the Continental Congress. This Congress had very little real power. However it did help the colonies work together. And it made George Washington a general to take command of the little American army.

TAUNTON FLAG

AN APPEAL TO HEAVEN

This army, which was camped outside Boston, was a strange little army indeed. The men had no training. Their guns were whatever they had brought from home. Some of them wore one kind of uniform, some another. Most of them had no uniform at all.

There was no official flag. Instead, the minutemen had dozens of flags, all different. There were flags from the different colonies and even from the different towns. The only flag the colonies had in common was that of Great Britain, the country they were fighting.

Washington's first job was to train his men. He taught them to drill, to build forts, and to fire cannon. He wrote to Congress asking for uniforms, more guns, and ammunition.

By January 1, 1776, the army was taking shape. To celebrate this, Washington raised a new flag over his camp. The men stared up at it, bright in the winter sunlight.

GADSDEN FLAG

DONT TREAD ON ME

BUNKER HILL FLAG

The British flag had a solid red field with a blue union. In the union were red and white crosses—red for England and white for Scotland. The crosses symbolized the union of England and Scotland. So the flag was sometimes called the Union Flag.

The flag Washington raised still had the crosses in the union. This showed that the colonies were still loyal to the British King. But the solid red field of the British flag was now divided into thirteen red and white stripes, for the thirteen united colonies.

This new flag came to be called the Great Union Flag. It was never adopted by Congress, but it came to be better known than any other American flag at that time.

Colonial banners fluttered gaily from the top of a
liberty pole at the very first Fourth of July celebration
of the Declaration of Independence.

2. The Flag Resolution

When Washington took command of his army, many Americans were still loyal to the British King. But gradually more and more persons came to believe the colonies should be independent. Finally, on July 4, 1776, the Declaration of Independence was adopted by Congress. Men on galloping horses spread the news. Great bonfires lit the night sky. A new nation, free and independent, was born— the United States of America.

The Great Union Flag, which symbolized loyalty to the British King, was no longer a suitable flag for Washington's army. Instead, many soldiers again used their local flags of many shapes and colors. Some had a picture of a pine tree, others, the picture of a rattlesnake. Many had one thing in common—thirteen stripes or thirteen stars to represent the thirteen colonies.

For a while the Continental Congress was too busy running the war to adopt a national flag. Finally, on June 14, 1777, an unknown member of Congress made the following suggestion:

"RESOLVED: that the flag of the United States be made of thirteen stripes, alternate red and white; that the union be thirteen stars, white in a blue field representing a new constellation."

One man who claimed that he made the suggestion was Francis Hopkinson. A poet and artist, he was a member of Congress when the design was adopted. Three years later Mr. Hopkinson wrote a letter to the United States Board of Admiralty. In it he listed several things that he said he had designed. The first was "the Flag of the United States of America."

Mr. Hopkinson said that he had never charged any money for his work. He asked, jokingly, if a quarter cask of wine would not be a proper reward.

A committee of Congress then considered Mr. Hopkinson's request. Finally they reported that Hopkinson "was not the only person consulted . . ." So Mr. Hopkinson never got his wine. Nor did he get official recognition as the man who designed the flag. However Mr. Hopkinson probably did help with the design.

It is easy to see how the new flag was created. It kept the thirteen stripes of the Great Union Flag, which stood for the thirteen colonies. The British crosses were removed from the union, and in their place now were thirteen white stars. Vermont and Rhode Island had already used stars in their local flags.

The flag resolution did not specify the shape of the flag. It did not say how the stars should be arranged or how many points they should have. It did not say whether the stripes should be vertical or horizontal. Nor did the government supply the army with the new flag. So few, if any, were used in land battles. Those that were used were made by hand and varied in design according to fancy, though the stripes, so far as we know, were always horizontal.

One of these early flags is still in existence at Bennington, Vermont. It has seven white stripes and six red stripes. In the union eleven stars form an arch

BENNINGTON FLAG

NORTH CAROLINA
MILITIA FLAG

POPULAR VERSION
OF THE FIRST
STARS AND STRIPES

over the figure "76." The other two stars are at the top corners of the union.

This flag may have been carried at the Battle of Bennington in 1777. In this battle a British force was marching toward Bennington when suddenly it came face to face with American soldiers. The British believed the newcomers were men loyal to the King. A British officer rode to greet them. He shouted, "Be ye King George's men?"

The American answer was to open fire. Before the battle was over more than half the British force had been killed or captured.

Another Revolutionary War flag that has been preserved is now in the North Carolina Hall of History in Raleigh. This flag has seven blue and six red stripes. The union is white with blue stars.

3. Early Flags at Sea

The use of flags or other national symbols is as old as history. Primitive people often painted their bodies before going into battle to show which side they were on. Or they might carry the skin of an animal tied to a tall pole.

A flag is even more important to a navy than to an army. It is often the only way that warships can identify one another.

Washington realized that his ships must have flags. In the early days of the Revolution, America built some armed schooners. Since no flag had been adopted, Washington's secretary wrote to the man outfitting the ships, "Please fix on some particular color for a flag and a signal by which our vessels may know one another. What do you think of a flag with a white ground and a green tree in the middle with the motto 'An Appeal to Heaven'?" This, the secretary said, was the flag used by Washington's small gunboats.

And this was the flag some American ships used until the Stars and Stripes was adopted by Congress.

Not long after the Flag Resolution, a young Navy officer named John Paul Jones went to sea in command of the armed sloop *Ranger*. With him he took the new flag. Flying it, he sailed into Quiberon Bay off the coast of France. The guns of the French fleet boomed a salute to the American flag. This was the first time a foreign nation had saluted the Stars and Stripes.

At sea again in April 1778, Jones sighted the British warship *Drake*. There was a short, fierce battle. The *Drake* was forced to surrender. It was the first time the Stars and Stripes was flown in battle at sea. It may have been the first time it was flown in battle anywhere. Unfortunately, we do not know exactly what the flag looked like.

A year later, the Stars and Stripes played an important role in the most famous naval battle of the Revolutionary War.

One evening two warships sailed side by side a few miles from the English coast. It was September 23, 1779. Sunset touched on the big British flags that each ship flew at its stern.

Captain Richard Pearson was commander of His Majesty's new frigate *Serapis*, which was escorting a group of merchant ships to England. At that time warships often flew the wrong flag to confuse the enemy. Captain Pearson did not believe the ship opposite him was really British. Using a speaking trumpet, he shouted, "What ship is that?"

On the other ship was an officer wearing a blue and white uniform. He was John Paul Jones, now a Commodore in the American Navy. Jones' ship, the *Bonhomme Richard*, had been given to the young nation by France. It was not as big or as fast as the *Serapis*, but the Commodore had decided to attack. John Paul Jones knew that in a fight his only chance of victory lay in getting close to the enemy. This was his reason for flying the British flag.

From the deck of the *Serapis* Captain Pearson shouted, "Answer immediately, or I shall fire into you!"

Jones gave his orders quickly. Down came the British flag. In its place rose a huge striped flag with white stars on a blue field in the corner. As the new flag unfurled in the wind, the *Bonhomme Richard* opened fire. In the same instant, the *Serapis'* guns boomed.

Both ships were hurt, but both continued to fire. Then two of the *Richard's* heaviest cannon burst. Many of her crew were killed. Now the *Richard* was less

The new American flag flies proudly at the stern of the *Bonhomme Richard* as she exchanges cannon fire with the British ship *Serapis*.

of a match for the *Serapis* than ever. But Jones did not turn away. Instead, he swung his ship toward the *Serapis* to ram her.

At this point Captain Pearson noticed that the American flag was gone. To strike the flag—to take it down in the course of a battle—was a sign of surrender. Actually, the American flag had been carried away by a shell. But Captain Pearson did not know this. He called to Jones, "Has your ship struck?"

John Paul Jones' answer has become an immortal part of naval history. "I have not yet begun to fight!" he shouted.

The *Bonhomme Richard* crashed into the *Serapis*. Quickly American sailors tied them together. With their cannon touching, the ships poured shells into one another. Soon both ships were afire.

Captain Pearson lost his nerve. With his own hands he hauled down the British flag as a sign of surrender.

The *Bonhomme Richard* was so badly battered that it sank soon after the battle. Before it did, John Paul Jones and his crew moved to the captured *Serapis*. Over the ship Jones raised another United States flag. Then he sailed off to a neutral Dutch harbor.

At this time the British government did not recognize the United States as an independent country. The British told the Dutch that the *Serapis* had been captured by pirates. John Paul Jones, the British said, had not fought under the flag of any recognized nation.

To settle the argument, the Dutch sent an artist to paint an exact picture of the *Serapis'* flag. The artist also painted a

These American flags were painted by an unknown
Dutch artist in 1779. The top flag was flown by the
American ship *Alliance* and the bottom flag by the
captured *Serapis*.

picture of the flag on the *Alliance*, another American warship anchored in the Dutch harbor. Today these pictures belong to the Chicago Historical Society. They are probably the oldest accurate pictures we have of the United States flag.

The *Serapis'* flag had stripes of red, white and blue. The *Alliance's* flag had no blue stripes, but it had seven white stripes and six red. The thirteen stars on the *Serapis'* flag were in three lines. The stars on the *Alliance's* flag were in five lines. Neither of these flags looked much like today's Stars and Stripes.

Although the design of these early flags varied, they stood for the same thing. They symbolized the new nation and the liberty and independence for which it was fighting.

4. Our Flag — Past and Present

After the Americans gained their independence, new states began to join the Union. By 1792 there were fifteen states. But the flag still had only thirteen stripes and thirteen stars.

A Congressman from Vermont, one of the new states, introduced a bill to change the flag. He wanted it to have fifteen stripes and fifteen stars. Other

Congressmen wanted it left as it was. Finally, the Congressman from Vermont won the argument. A bill was passed saying the flag should have fifteen stars, and fifteen stripes. There was still no rule on how they should be placed.

As time went by more states entered the Union. Soon there were twenty in all. But there were still only fifteen stars in the flag, and fifteen stripes. Some people wanted to add a new star for each state, along with a new stripe. Others said this would soon make the flag look like a barber's pole. They wanted to go back to thirteen stripes and thirteen stars. Since everyone disagreed, flags were made to suit each person.

On December 16, 1817 a Congressman named Peter Wendover made a speech in Congress. He said he had counted the

stripes in the flag over the nearby Navy Yard. It had nine stripes. Then he had counted the stripes in the flag over the Capitol building. It had eighteen stripes. Mr. Wendover asked Congress to decide just what the flag should be.

Congress was slow to act. But on April 4, 1818 a new law went into effect. It said that the flag should have thirteen horizontal stripes representing the thirteen original colonies. However, there should be one star in the union for each state. Whenever a new state was admitted to the Union, a new star would be added on the following Fourth of July.

There was not one word in the law about the placement of the stars. The first new flag was flown over the Capitol Building. It had 20 stars placed in the shape of one big star!

President James Monroe didn't like this star-shaped design. He thought the stars should be placed in parallel rows. Some flag makers, however, continued to do as they pleased. Stars were placed in a diamond, a circle, and even an anchor!

It was not until 1912—135 years after the Flag Resolution of 1777—that the

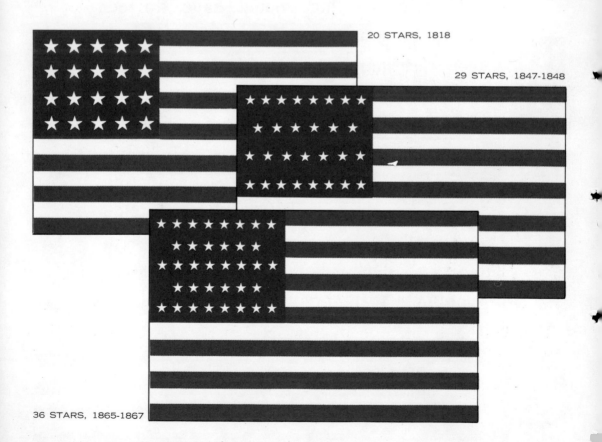

20 STARS, 1818

29 STARS, 1847-1848

36 STARS, 1865-1867

position of the stars was finally settled. That year President William Howard Taft ordered that they should always be in parallel lines.

At that time there were 48 states in the union and 48 stars in the flag. During World War II America began to realize the importance of the territories

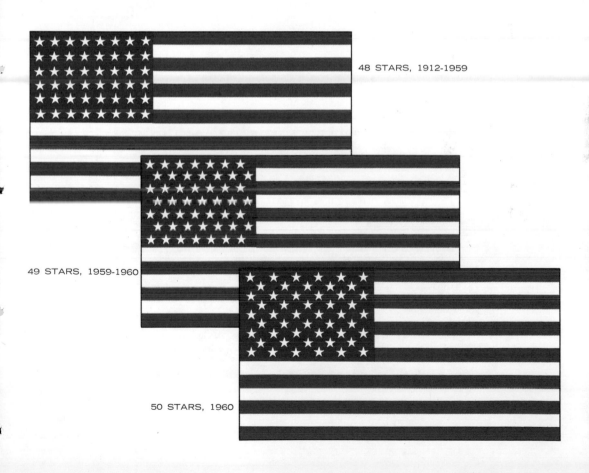

48 STARS, 1912-1959

49 STARS, 1959-1960

50 STARS, 1960

of Alaska and Hawaii. So in 1959, first Alaska and then Hawaii became states.

Each time, President Eisenhower issued a rule fixing the new order of the stars. When there were forty-nine states, the stars were in seven rows of seven stars each. Now with 50 states in the Union, the stars are in nine rows. Five of the rows have six stars each. The four alternate rows have five stars each.

Our fifty states (in gold) reach far beyond the original thirteen states in 1776 (in green).

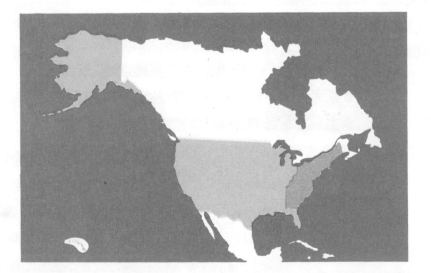

5. "And the Rocket's Red Glare..."

During the early days of the United States there was not much interest in the national flag. Because the nation was new, many people felt more loyal to their home state than to the nation. The state flags seemed more important than the Stars and Stripes. Then in 1812 the United States went to war with England for the second time. During this war something happened that made people deeply conscious and proud of their national flag.

The War of 1812 did not start well for the United States. British troops captured Washington, D.C., the nation's capital. Here they arrested an American doctor named William Beanes. He was taken to one of the British warships in Chesapeake Bay.

Dr. Beanes had a friend named Francis Scott Key, a lawyer who liked to write poetry. When Key heard of Beanes' arrest, he went in a small boat to the ship where Beanes was held. He asked the British admiral to set Dr. Beanes free.

Finally the Admiral agreed. "However," he said, "I cannot let either you or Dr. Beanes go ashore now. We are going to attack Baltimore. I will have to hold you prisoner until the fight is over."

The British fleet sailed up the Bay. At daylight on September 13, 1814, it lay in the harbor outside Baltimore, Maryland. Between the fleet and the city was Fort McHenry. Over the fort waved an American flag.

It was a huge flag, 42 feet long and 30 feet wide, with fifteen red and white stripes. From the deck of the British ship, Key watched the great flag ripple in the morning breeze. His heart beat proudly at the sight.

One of the British ships flashed a signal. An instant later the guns of the fleet began to roar. The ship on which Key was held prisoner did not join in the fighting. But from it Key could see the British shells striking the fort. He could see the flash of the American guns in return.

A shell tore through the huge flag.

Flying splinters ripped it. But still the flag waved in the wind. Key knew that, as long as the flag was there, the fort was in American hands.

The battle went on all day and into the night. By the flash of the exploding shells, Key could see the flag.

Sometime during the night it began to rain. Key could no longer see the flag, or tell how the battle was going. But still he stood in the rain, watching and listening.

Toward dawn the rain stopped. The firing stopped too. The battle was over, but who had won?

Daylight came slowly. Fog lay low over the water. Sometimes, when the fog parted, Key could see the fort. There was a flag—but he could not tell what flag. Then a slanting beam of sunlight

"At dawn's early light," Francis Scott Key hailed the
Star Spangled Banner still flying over Fort McHenry.
Painting by Percy Moran.

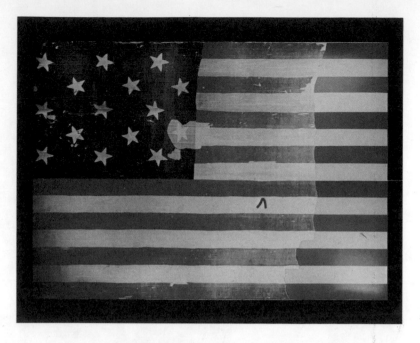

The great flag that flew over Fort McHenry is now at the Smithsonian Institution, Washington, D.C.

touched on the banner, and the colors glowed in the light.

It was the Stars and Stripes! The British ships were turning away. The Americans had won!

Deeply moved by what he had seen, Francis Scott Key wrote a poem. He did not name it, but it was soon called "The Star Spangled Banner."

Oh, say, can you see by the dawn's
early light
What so proudly we hailed at the twi-
light's last gleaming?
Whose broad stripes and bright stars,
through the perilous fight,
O'er the ramparts we watched were so
gallantly streaming.
And the rocket's red glare, the bombs
bursting in air,
Gave proof through the night that
our flag was still there.
Oh, say, does that Star Spangled Ban-
ner yet wave
O'er the land of the free and the
home of the brave?

Set to an old popular tune, "The Star
Spangled Banner" was soon being sung all
over the country. Today it is the official
National Anthem of the United States.

Northern soldiers rushed into action at the Battle of
Fredericksburg proudly carrying the Stars and Stripes.
Painting by Frederick Cavada.

6. The Flag in the Civil War

During the Civil War the Stars and Stripes waved over battlefields where Northern soldiers fought those from the South. In 1861, soon after the Southern states had seceded, the flag had 34 stars. The federal government made no change in the number of stars. They said the Southern states had no right to secede.

The Confederacy, however, wanted a flag of its own. The first one had two broad red stripes with one white stripe in the middle. The union was blue with seven white stars in a circle. These stood for the seven states that had left the federal government.

From a distance, this flag looked very much like the flag of the United States. During the First Battle of Bull Run, these similar flags caused trouble. Some Union soldiers saw a flag partly hidden by the smoke of the guns. They thought it was the Stars and Stripes and ran to join their friends. Suddenly they realized it was the Confederate Flag and they were in hand-to-hand battle. Another time Confederate soldiers mistook their flag for that of the enemy and turned their guns on their own soldiers.

After this battle Confederate generals decided they must have a new flag. It was designed by General P. G. T. Beauregard.

It had a red field, with a white-bordered blue cross which ran from corner to corner. In the cross were thirteen white stars. These stood for the thirteen states expected to join the Confederacy. Actually only eleven states did.

This flag was called the Southern Cross. Rippling in the wind, it often seemed to be all red. It was carried in most Civil War battles, including that of Gettysburg.

Gettysburg was the most important battle of the war. For three days gray-

THE STARS AND BARS
(First Confederate National Flag)

THE SOUTHERN CROSS
(Confederate Battle Flag)

uniformed men carrying the Southern Cross charged against the blue-clad soldiers beneath the Stars and Stripes. The biggest fight of all was on the third day. The Southern troops of General George Pickett charged the Union forces on top

Confederate battle flags rippled bravely over the Southern soldiers who attacked Union lines on the first day of the Battle of Gettysburg.

of a hill called Cemetery Ridge. On this fight hung the fate of the battle and, quite possibly, the nation. Later, one of the Union soldiers described the charge.

From the top of Cemetery Ridge, the soldier wrote, "every eye could see . . . an ocean of armed men sweeping toward us! . . . More than half a mile their front extends; and more than a thousand yards the dull gray masses deploy, man touching man. The red flags wave, their horsemen gallop up and down; the arms of 18,000 men . . . gleam in the sun. . . ."

Behind the Union lines, according to the same soldier: "The colors of the brigades and divisions move to their places in the rear; but along the lines in front, the grand old ensign . . . stood up, and the west wind kissed it as the sergeants sloped its lance toward the enemy. I believe that there was not one above whom it then waved . . . whose heart did not swell with pride toward it."

As the Southern soldiers charged up the

hill, artillery and rifle fire cut them down. Flag bearers fell. Other men caught up the flags and rushed on. But the gray lines grew thinner and the flags, fewer.

A few reached the top of the hill. For a short time the Southern Cross and the Stars and Stripes waved side by side. And then the Southern flags disappeared. Some were ripped apart by bullets; others fell as the flag bearers were killed. The last of the Southern troops went reeling back down the hill.

The battle that did more to save the Union than any other was over. And on top of Cemetery Ridge, the Stars and Stripes still waved.

Many of the soldiers killed in the Battle of Gettysburg were buried near where they fell. A few months later President Abraham Lincoln came there to dedicate

the ground as a national cemetery. Beside him waved the Stars and Stripes.

"Four score and seven years ago," the President said, "our fathers brought forth on this continent a new nation, conceived in liberty and dedicated to the proposition that all men are created equal."

The listening crowd watched the flag waving beside the tall, bearded President. They had to strain to hear his words.

". . . we here highly resolve that these dead shall not have died in vain; that this nation, under God, shall have a new birth of freedom; and that government of the people, by the people, for the people, shall not perish from the earth."

President Lincoln lived to see the end of the tragic war. Then, a few days later, he was murdered by a madman.

While the whole nation grieved, the

body of the President was taken from Washington to his home in Illinois. All along the way, across the entire nation, flags hung at half-mast in mourning.

Today flags are often used to cover the caskets of soldiers and government leaders. Lincoln's casket was draped in black cloth. But at each end, three flags hung limp against their staffs.

It was during the Civil War that the name Old Glory began to be widely used for the United States flag. According to story, the name was given to the flag by a man named William Driver in the 1830's. Captain Driver was a merchant seaman. Wherever he went, his ship always flew a flag that had been given to him by his mother. He called it Old Glory.

When William Driver was an old man, he left the sea and settled in Nashville,

Tennessee. Here Old Glory flew day after day over Driver's home. Then in 1861 Tennessee seceded from the Union. The Civil War began. Captain Driver was loyal to the Union. But he knew that if he tried to fly Old Glory, it would be torn down by the Confederates. So he kept it carefully hidden inside a mattress cover.

In 1862 the Union soldiers captured Nashville. Quickly William Driver took his flag from its hiding place and went to the State Capitol Building. Stiffly he climbed to the dome and fastened Old Glory to the flagstaff. "Thank God," he said, "I have lived to raise Old Glory over the Capitol of Tennessee."

Just how accurate the story is we do not know. But the name for the flag became popular. The United States flag is still called Old Glory today.

7. Flag Day
   and Two World Wars

In the spring of 1916 the shadow of World War I was spreading over America. People knew that before long the United States might be drawn into the fight already raging in Europe.

The thought of war made the American people more aware of their freedom. To save this freedom, both at home and abroad, they were willing to go to war.

The American flag stood as a proud symbol of freedom and justice. For years people had wanted a holiday to honor the flag. Now President Woodrow Wilson issued a proclamation. He said that every June 14 should be "observed as Flag Day with special patriotic exercises" in every town and city. It was on June 14, 1777 that Congress had first adopted the Stars and Stripes.

On June 14, 1916 Flag Day was celebrated as a national holiday for the first time. School children colored pictures of the flag, read stories about it, and recognized the flag as a symbol of their country. Soldiers, Boy Scouts, and other patriotic groups marched in parades. Bands played. Speakers told of heroes who had brought honor to their flag.

In 1917, one year after the observance of Flag Day, the United States entered World War I. American soldiers were sent to help the French people defend their country against the Germans. They took the Stars and Stripes with them. It waved above the men as they marched off the ships and through the French cities. There were not many soldiers in these first units to reach France. But to the French people the sight of the flag was more important than the number of men. For the flag symbolized the total power of the United States and the willingness of its people to fight for freedom.

Twenty-three years after the end of World War I, the Japanese bombed Pearl Harbor and brought the United States into World War II. Many American ships were sunk that day. Later most of them were raised and repaired so they could once again fly the flag in battle. But the battleship *Arizona* was beyond repair. It rested on the bottom of the harbor, only a small bit of its hull above the surface. But a flag was soon fastened to that steel skeleton. It has been flying above the *Arizona* ever since, in memory of the men who were killed in the attack.

During the war American fighting men carried Old Glory to Europe and across the Pacific. It waved over hundreds of battles. The best known battle photograph of the flag was taken on Iwo Jima, a tiny island south of Japan. Here one of the most desperate battles of the war was fought.

At the south end of the island is an old volcano called Mt. Suribachi. Around this volcano the fighting was particularly fierce. At last United States Marines reached the top. While Japanese shells burst around them, they raised a small

A news photographer took this famous picture of Marines raising the American flag on the hard-won island of Iwo Jima.

American flag. As they did so, a Marine photographer took their picture. A hand grenade burst near the photographer, and he fell 50 feet down the side of the volcano. His camera was smashed, but he saved the film.

Strangely enough, none of his pictures looked very exciting.

Later more Marines raised a still larger flag. They, too, were under fire. Still another photographer took their picture. This one caught all the excitement of the action. It showed the pride the soldiers felt for their flag.

Before long the picture was printed in newspapers all over the country. It became the most famous picture of World War II. It was used on a stamp and reproduced in a huge statue—the Marine Corps Memorial in Arlington, Virginia.

8. The Flag in Peace

Most Americans see their flag almost every day. It waves over homes, schools, and government buildings. Because we see it so often we usually pay no special attention to it. But to the early immigrants arriving in this country, their first sight of the Stars and Stripes was never forgotten. The flag stood for a new life in a new world, for religious and political freedom, justice, and opportunity.

As the new nation spread westward, the United States flag went with it. Pioneers crossing the Allegheny Mountains sometimes painted the flag on their Conestoga wagons. Boatmen drifting down the Ohio and Mississippi Rivers carried crude, handmade flags.

In 1803 President Thomas Jefferson purchased the Louisiana Territory from France. This included nearly all the land between the Mississippi River and the Rocky Mountains. It doubled the size of the country over which the Stars and Stripes could fly. To mark the change in ownership, a ceremony was held in the public square in New Orleans.

Although the Louisiana Territory was bought from France, Spain had previously owned it. On December 20, 1803, the Spanish flag was raised to the top of the

The French flag came down; the Stars and Stripes
went up; and Louisiana became part of the United
States. Painting by T. de Thulstrup.

pole in the public square. Slowly it was lowered, folded, and taken away. Then the French flag was raised. It too was lowered and folded. Then, briskly, the Stars and Stripes went up to stay.

When the pioneer wagon trains moved still further west, the Stars and Stripes went with them. It waved over lonely military posts on the Great Plains. It reached the Pacific Ocean when California and the Oregon Territory became part of the United States. Eventually it would fly over Alaska and Hawaii.

Wherever United States citizens have gone exploring, the flag has gone with them. In 1898 a naval officer named Robert E. Peary set out to reach the North Pole. Before he left home his wife gave him a silk flag she had made. Peary promised to raise it at the North Pole.

For three summers Peary kept trying to reach the Pole. Each time he was turned back by fierce storms, hunger, or great gaps in the polar ice. Once his feet were frozen and seven toes had to be amputated. Each time he was forced back he cut a small piece from the flag he carried, and buried it in the snow to mark how far north he had gone. Each summer he went farther.

In 1906 Peary tried again to reach the Pole. This time he came within 175 miles of his goal. Again he left a small piece of the flag to mark his progress.

Finally, on April 6, 1909 Robert Peary, a Negro assistant named Matthew Henson, and four Eskimos became the first men ever to reach the North Pole.

Peary raised the tattered flag he had carried for so long. Briefly it waved in

the icy air. Then Peary lowered it. He cut one final piece to bury in the snow. He wrapped the rest around his body to take home again.

Nineteen years later another United States Naval officer, Richard E. Byrd, led an expedition to the Antarctic. When a great wall of ice blocked his ships, Byrd and his party moved inland by dog sled and tractor to set up a base called Little America. From here on November 29, 1929, he took off in an airplane to fly over the South Pole. There he dropped the Stars and Stripes as a symbol of United States achievement.

Today when astronauts boom off into space, the flag is sewn on their suits. It is on the satellites that circle the earth and on the space ships that land upon the moon. Sailors in submarines have planted the flag on the bottom of the ocean, thousands of feet below the surface.

Wherever the flag goes, into space or in a parade along a city street, it stands for the nation and the people who love it. Perhaps this was best said in a poem by Henry Holcomb Bennett:

Hats off!
Along the street there comes
A blare of bugles, a ruffle of drums,
A flash of color beneath the sky:
Hats off!
The flag is passing by!

Blue and crimson and white it shines,
Over the steel-tipped ordered lines.
Hats off!
The colors before us fly;
But more than the flag is passing by:

Sea-fights and land-fights, grim and great,
Fought to make and save the State:
Weary marches and sinking ships;
Cheers of victory on dying lips;

Days of plenty and years of peace;
March of a strong land's swift increase;
Equal justice, right and law;
Stately honor and reverend awe;

Sign of a nation great and strong
To ward her people from foreign wrong:
Pride and glory and honor—all
Live in the colors to stand or fall.

Along the street there comes
A blare of bugles, a ruffle of drums,
A flash of color beneath the sky:
             Hats off!
The flag is passing by!

HOW TO DISPLAY
THE FLAG

1: The flag is usually displayed only between sunrise and sunset. On special occasions it may be shown at night for patriotic effect.

2: During school days the flag should be flown on or near every schoolhouse.

3: To fly the flag at half-mast is a sign of mourning. On Memorial Day the flag is flown at half-mast until noon, then raised.

4: In a parade, the American flag should be carried on the right of other flags in the same line or in the center if it is carried ahead of another line of flags.

5: On crossed staffs with another flag, the Stars and Stripes should be on the other flag's right (the left of the person looking toward the flag). Its staff should be in front of the other staff.

6: On the same staff with a state or city flag, the Stars and Stripes should be at the peak.

7: Displayed on the wall, the flag should be flat with the union in the upper left corner.

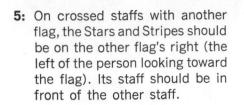

8: If the flags of two or more nations are flown together, they should be on separate staffs, at the same height, and about the same size.

9: All persons should stand at attention and salute when the flag is being raised, or lowered, or passing in a parade. Persons in uniform (soldiers, Boy Scouts, etc.) should give their proper salute. Men not in uniform remove their hats and hold them over their hearts with their right hands. Men not wearing hats hold their right hands over their hearts. Women salute in the same way, but without removing their hats.